T0193079

# The HANDBOOK for COMPANIONING the MOURNER

# The HANDBOOK for COMPANIONING the MOURNER

## Eleven Essential Principles

Alan D. Wolfelt, Ph.D.

Companion Press is an imprint of the Center for Loss and Life Transition,
3735 Broken Bow Road, Fort Collins, Colorado 80526, (970) 226-6050,
www.centerforloss.com.

Companion Press books may be purchased in bulk for sales promotions,
premiums and fundraisers.  Please contact the publisher at the above address for
more information.

Printed in the United States of America.

23  22                                        5  4  3

ISBN 978-1-879651-61-6

*To the heart-based caregivers who have traveled to my retreat-oriented training center to explore these "companioning" tenets with me in the sacred space of hospitality and sanctuary. I thank you for advocating for this model of care throughout the world.*

*Companion Press is dedicated to the education and support of both the bereaved and bereavement caregivers. We believe that those who companion the bereaved by walking with them as they journey in grief have a wondrous opportunity: to help others embrace and grow through grief—and to lead fuller, more deeply-lived lives themselves because of this important ministry.*

For a complete catalog and ordering information,

write or call or visit our website:

Companion
P R E S S

Companion Press
The Center for Loss and Life Transition
3735 Broken Bow Road
Fort Collins, CO 80526
(970) 226-6050  FAX 1-800-922-6051
DrWolfelt@centerforloss.com
www.centerforloss.com

# Contents

# Introduction

"Why not go out on a limb?
That is where the fruit is." —Will Rogers

## Why This Handbook?

I wrote eleven tenets of companioning people in grief several years ago as I sat in a gazebo on the sacred grounds of the Center for Loss and Life Transition. I am very humbled that today there is now an international network of both professional caregivers and laypeople who have trained with me on the companioning philosophy of caregiving.

While I had been teaching the art of companioning for many years, I initially published the eleven tenets of companioning in my 2006 book *Companioning the Bereaved: A Soulful Guide for Caregivers*, which also includes a section on counseling "how-tos." This Handbook is in response to a request for a more concise guide to the eleven tenets of companioning. I hope you will help me get both these resources into the hands and hearts of anyone you believe might benefit from learning more about creating hospitality for fellow human beings encountering grief.

## The Distinction Between "Treat" and "Companion"

I've always found it intriguing that the word "treat" comes from the Latin root word *tractare*, which means "to drag." If you combine that with the word "patient," we really get into trouble. "Patient" means "passive, long-term sufferer," so if we treat patients, we drag passive, long-term sufferers. Not a very empowering concept.

On the other hand, the word "companion," when broken down into its original Latin roots, means "messmate": *com* for "with" and *pan* for "bread." Someone you would share a meal with, a friend, an equal. That is the image of companioning—sitting at a table together, being present to one another, sharing, communing, abiding in the fellowship of hospitality.

I have taken liberties with the noun "companion" and made it into the verb "companioning" because it so well captures the type of counseling relationship I support and advocate. Instead of treating patients, I advocate companioning those who mourn. Companioning the bereaved is not about assessing, analyzing, fixing, or resolving another's grief. Instead, it is about being totally present to the mourner, even being a temporary guardian of her soul.

# Treatment vs. Companioning
## For Spiritual, Emotional, Existential Issues

Treatment Model

- Tries to return the mourner to a prior state of homeostatic balance ("old normal").

- Control or stop distressful symptoms; distress is bad.

- Follows a prescriptive model where counselor is perceived as expert.

- Pathology rooted in sustained relationship to dead person.

- Positions the griever in a passive role.

- Grieving person ranges from compliant to noncompliant.

- Quality of care judged by how well grief was "managed."

- Denial interferes with efficient integration of the loss and must be overcome.

- Establish control; create strategic plan of intervention.

- Provide satisfactory answers for all emotional, spiritual questions and dilemmas.

Companioning Model

- Emphasizes the transformative, life-changing experience of grief ("new normal").

- Observe, "watch out for," "bear witness," and see value in soul-based symptoms of grief.

- Bereaved person guides the journey; "teach me" is the foundational principle.

- Is a normal shift from relationship of presence to relationship of memory.

- Recognizes the need for mourner to actively mourn.

- Grieving person expresses the reality of being "torn apart" as best he can.

- Quality of care monitored by how well we allowed the griever to lead the journey.

- Denial helps sustain the integration of the loss from head to heart. It is matched with patience and compassion.

- Show up with curiosity; willingness to learn from the griever.

- Honor the mystery; facilitate the continuing "search for meaning"; no urgency to solve or satisfy the dilemma.

## Do You Need to be an "Expert"?

Before we begin this journey together, you have the right to know what motivates and inspires me to advocate for this companioning philosophy of caring for people in grief. In my workshops across North America, I often say, "It is not so much what is new in grief care; it is what we once had and have lost." Perhaps instead of creating new scientific theories (that are often secular, ego-centered, and "expert"-based), we would be better serving our fellow human beings if we realized that every person is called upon to be a healer. As a "responsible rebel," I cannot accept the all-too-common projected mandate from many mental health practitioners that compassionate grief care must be limited to the domain of the "certified specialist."

**Responsible Rebel:** One who questions assumptive models surrounding grief and loss and challenges those very models. Rebels are not afraid to question established structures and forms. At the same time, rebels respect the rights of others to use different models of understanding, and provide leadership in ways that empower people rather than diminish them. So, if the contents of this book resonate with you, please join me in being a responsible rebel!

As Henri Nouwen astutely observed, "Healing means, first of all, the creation of an empty but friendly space. Where those who suffer can tell their story to someone who can listen with real attention." We must ask ourselves as caregivers: Are we going to limit the care of mourners to "certified thanatologists"? Or, can we recognize that many people can create sacred space and companion their fellow human beings?

After all, the active work of mourning is the domain of the person experiencing grief and loss. Our caregiving role is to travel alongside as a hospitable companion on the sacred journey. We are responsible *to* the mourner, not *for* the mourner.

Those who are vested in maintaining the current image of the need for "certified" grief care providers may question the companioning model outlined in this Handbook. People who have achieved a measure of status and authority often dislike having their legitimacy questioned.

Some people, whether they have a vested interest or not, may take issue with the belief that laypeople can artfully companion others in grief. Again, look backward. Before the advent of the specialist and the evolution of our mourning-avoidant culture, people turned to their neighbors and friends for support and compassion. The need to retell your story of love and loss was perceived as a necessary rite of passage. But now people have moved from the front porch, where they were supported in the need to mourn, to the privacy of the back porch, where they risk keeping their grief internalized. And, if they do need help, they are encouraged to go see a "grief expert."

Perhaps what matters is not that I am right in this belief, but rather that I stimulate more conversation about the trend toward limiting the care of mourners to "specialists." My hope is that this book creates more of that conversation.

## Creating a Safe Place

Perhaps the ministry of caring for mourners would change dramatically if we thought of our work more as providing an ongoing safe place of care than as leading people to resolution or recovery. Superficial techniques focused on restoring a prior state of "normal" and getting people to "let go" and achieve "closure" result in more harm than good. Artful companioning requires different semantics than that of psychological-based therapies and interventions.

Companioning sees another reality than the need to eliminate what are often termed "negative emotions." It appreciates that new life is born out of befriending pain and suffering. While generally devalued in our society, the painful emotions of grief have a wisdom of their own that are essential to the work of mourning.

Actually, companions are "hospitality hosts" who patiently listen to love stories. In the telling of the stories, mourners befriend their grief and slowly, with no rewards for speed, transform their suffering. Yes, Kierkegaard was right: "While life must eventually be lived forward, it is understood and made meaning of backward."

I recently met a very educated psychologist who told me that he could never do the work I do, journeying alongside people who are in deep grief, because he, in such work, would feel so very helpless. I tried as best I could to help him understand that we all have different callings, but I also attempted to help him understand that companioning people in grief is not undertaken by some remarkable element of society who befriend the pain and suffering of grief with serene confidence. Those of us who companion mourners do indeed feel helpless. And there is good reason—*because we are helpless.* There is no anesthetizing the pain of grief that comes with the death of someone loved.

Any kind of "expert" model of grief care runs into trouble when feelings of helplessness are encountered by the caregiver. After all, helplessness is not what the expert aspires to. In fact, it is what he or she runs away FROM. Helplessness is in opposition to expertise. As a consequence, techniques used to treat the patient instinctively combat helplessness and attempt to eradicate soul-based symptoms of loss (e.g., depression, anxiety, chaos, confusion, loss of control). It requires little reflection to understand that this approach breaks down and actually creates distance between the caregiver and the mourner.

Those caregivers who don't run away from their helplessness have learned that their willingness to embrace uncertainty is a gift to those experiencing grief. Their acceptance of helplessness in themselves and in others disarms any felt need to be the "expert." At the mourner's side, the caregiver learns to observe, to watch out for, to keep and honor, and to bear witness. The companion learns the value of sitting in silence, being still, waiting, listening with the heart, and not being attached to outcome! Yes, companioning requires humility rather than expertise, and surrender rather than control.

If you desire to support fellow human beings in grief, you must create a safe place for people to embrace their feelings of profound loss. This safe place is not a physical space but rather a cleaned-out, compassionate heart. It is the open heart and befriending of your helplessness that allow you to be truly present to another human being's intimate pain. An awareness of the need to learn (as opposed to the need to be the expert) is the essence of true companioning.

I truly believe we are all here to, in part, love and care for those our lives touch—each of us in his own way. Supporting my fellow human beings in grief nourishes my soul. Likewise, if you are dedicated to caring for—not curing—people in grief, you are nourishing your own soul and the souls of those you touch. May you find inspiration and hope in the pages that follow.

Sincerely,

Alan D. Wolfelt

# The Tenets of Companioning the Bereaved

**Tenet One**  Companioning is about being present to another person's pain; it is not about taking away the pain.

**Tenet Two**  Companioning is about going to the wilderness of the soul with another human being; it is not about thinking you are responsible for finding the way out.

**Tenet Three**  Companioning is about honoring the spirit; it is not about focusing on the intellect.

**Tenet Four**  Companioning is about listening with the heart; it is not about analyzing with the head.

**Tenet Five**  Companioning is about bearing witness to the struggles of others; it is not about judging or directing these struggles.

**Tenet Six**  Companioning is about walking alongside; it is not about leading.

**Tenet Seven**  Companioning is about discovering the gifts of sacred silence; it does not mean filling up every moment with words.

**Tenet Eight**  Companioning is about being still; it is not about frantic movement forward.

**Tenet Nine**  Companioning is about respecting disorder and confusion; it is not about imposing order and logic.

**Tenet Ten**  Companioning is about learning from others; it is not about teaching them.

**Tenet Eleven**  Companioning is about compassionate curiosity; it is not about expertise.

## Tenet One

# Companioning is about being present to another person's pain; it is not about taking away the pain.

*"In every heart there is an inner room, where we can hold our greatest treasures and our deepest pain."* —Marianne Williamson

To be bereaved literally means to be "torn apart." When someone is torn apart, there is a natural need to embrace the heartfelt pain of the loss. There is no pill we can take to relieve the pain and suffering, and no surgery that can reassemble the pieces of a broken heart. The way in which we care for fellow humans who are suffering the pain of loss has much to do with the ways in which we will be able to supportively companion others.

> "The word care implies a way of responding to expressions of the soul that is not heroic and muscular."
> —Thomas Moore

Sadly, current North American culture often makes the person in grief feel intense shame and embarrassment about feelings of pain and suffering. People who are perceived as "doing well" with their grief are considered "strong" and "under control." Society erroneously implies that if grieving people openly express feelings of pain and suffering, they are immature or overly emotional.

> "Man could not live if he were entirely impervious to sadness. Many sorrows can be endured only by being embraced... Melancholy is morbid only when it occupies too much place in life; but it is equally morbid for it to be wholly excluded from life."
> —Emile Durkheim

14

**Courage**
The word courage comes from the French word for heart (*coeur*).
Courage grows for those things in life that impact us deeply. The
death of someone treasured opens, or engages, our hearts. Then
we must take our hearts, which have been engaged, and muster
the courage to encounter any and all feelings, including pain and
suffering. Courage can also be defined as the ability to do what
one believes is right, despite the fact that others may strongly and
persuasively disagree.

In contemporary North American culture, pain and feelings of
loss are experiences most people try to avoid. Why? Because
the role of suffering is misunderstood. Normal thoughts and
feelings that result from loss are typically seen as unnecessary
and inappropriate. Yet, only in gathering courage to move
toward this hurt is anyone able to ultimately heal.

## Grief is not Shameful

As the bereaved experience grief, they are often greeted with
what I call "buck-up therapy"—messages like "carry on,"
"keep your chin up," or "just keep busy." And combined with
these messages is often another unstated but strong belief:
"You have a right not to hurt—so do whatever is necessary to

avoid it." In sum, people in grief are often encouraged to deny, avoid, or numb themselves to the pain of the experience.

When personal feelings of grief are met with shame-based messages or silent indifference, discovering how to integrate the loss becomes all but impossible. If

*"It is possible, in fact, to validate someone's feelings while at the same time validating their capacity to move beyond those feelings."* —Marianne Williamson

bereaved people internalize stated and unstated messages that encourage the repression, avoidance, or numbing of grief, they often become powerless to help themselves. I often say that finding the way into and through grief is often more difficult than finding a way beyond it. In fact, internalizing the belief that mourning is wrong or bad tempts many people to act as if they feel better than they really do. Ultimately, denying the grief denies one of the essences of life and puts one at risk for living in the "shadow of the ghosts of grief."

When we as caregivers experience the pain and suffering of a fellow human being, we instinctively want to take the pain away. Yet, to truly companion another human being requires that we sit with the pain as we overcome the instinct to want

16

to "fix." We may discover that we want to fix another's pain because it is hurting us too much.

Suffering doesn't mean something is wrong. It isn't happening because we made the wrong move or said the wrong thing. As Thomas

Moore wisely noted, "The basic intention of any caring—physical or psychological—is to alleviate suffering. But in relation to the symptom itself, observance means first of all listening and looking carefully at what is being revealed in the suffering. An intent to heal can get in the way of seeing. By doing less, more is accomplished."

Ultimately, if we rush in to take away a person's grief pain, we also take away the opportunity for her to integrate the loss into her life. To be truly a healing presence, we must be able to share another person's pain while realizing there is nothing we can do to instantly relieve it and knowing that we are not responsible for it—all the while seeking to empathetically understand what the pain feels like. The paradox of entering into the pain lies in the truth that as you affirm someone's feelings of suffering, you are also affirming his eventual capacity to move beyond those feelings. As Helen Keller taught us years ago, "The only way to the other side is through."

## The Wisdom of the Soul

Yes, sometimes it may seem as if you are "doing" very little as you open your heart to a fellow struggler. And yet this is an example of how companioning inspires an attribute of the soul: wisdom. Wisdom is the sense of recognizing that in your helplessness you ultimately become helpful. A wise caregiver will have the wisdom to know what she can do, accept what she can't do, and have the spirit of the heart engaged in ways

### Soullessness and the Divine Spark

In my experience, soul is real, authentic, and vital. When a mourner says, "I'm not sure I want to go on living," she is expressing a loss of her authenticity, her vitality. She is expressing what I call "soullessness." Part of the role of the companion is to be patiently present to her in ways that stir the vital force within her and help her discover renewed connection to the greater world of humanity. Companioning is, in part, the conduit through which the mourner can search for and find what Meister Eckhart termed the "divine spark"—that which gives depth and purpose to our living. What an honor to help relight the divine spark!

that can and do make a difference.

In providing a soulful response to another person's pain, we must discover and nurture two qualities that are within us: humility and "unknowing." We must first be present with an open mind and an open heart. To be open in this way of being is not an absence of thought, however. In fact, it is a clear, focused attentiveness to the moment. It is about immediacy—being present in the here and now.

When we as caregivers focus the power of our attention on the suffering of another human being, the full measure of our soul becomes available to her. Releasing any preconceptions of the need to take away pain allows our hearts to open wide and be infinitely more present, loving, and compassionate. Presence in the fullness of the moment is where the soul resides.

And being present to people in the pain of their grief is about being present to them in their "soul work." There is a lovely Jungian distinction between "soul work" and "spirit work."

*Soul work*: a downward movement in the psyche; a willingness to connect with what is dark, deep, and not necessarily pleasant.

*Spirit work*: a quality of moving toward the light; upward, ascending.

In part, being present to others' pain of grief is about being willing to descend with them into their soul work—which precedes their spirit work. A large part of being present to someone in soul work is to bear witness to the pain and suffering and not to think of it as a door to someplace else. This can help keep you in the moment. Dark, deep, and unpleasant emotions need to be held in the same way happiness and joy need to be held—with respect and humility.

## Acknowledging Our Own Suffering

As our hearts begin to open to the presence of suffering, challenging thoughts may creep in. Can I really help this person? Is the pain of his loss touching my own losses? If I reach out to support, what will happen to me? In the push-pull this experience triggers, there is little wonder that being present to the suffering of others seems so difficult.

The capacity to acknowledge our own discomfort when confronted with suffering is usually less overwhelming when it is no longer minimized or denied. To give attention to our helplessness can free us to open more fully to another as well as to our own pain and suffering. We no longer find ourselves wanting to run away. We can slow down, be still, and open to the presence of the pain. We can witness what *is* without feeling the need to fix it!

When we become conscious that any part of us wants to run away from the pain, we can gently embrace it; an entire new level of receptiveness becomes possible. As we become the companion, we begin to see what is being asked of us that is not so much about "doing" but instead about "being." We discover what anxieties and fears might be inhibiting our helping hearts, and come to trust the healing power of presence.

Finally, we can begin to listen—truly listen and give honor to the pain. Instead of pushing away suffering or merely releasing the need to "fix" it, we are able to enter into it. We are not indifferent or passive; we are fully available and open. We are truly being hospitable to the pain of another person.

In opening to our own suffering from life losses, we enhance our desire to be of service to those around us. We become truly available at deeper levels of our souls. We do not deny pain but open to it and learn what it is trying to teach us. In becoming more sensitive and responsive to one's own pain as well as the pain of others, we continue to see ourselves as students always learning to become more heartfelt companions to our fellow strugglers. What an honor!

# Tenet Two

Companioning is about going to the wilderness of the soul with another human being; it is not about thinking you are responsible for finding the way out.

*"The only map that does the spiritual traveler any good is the one that leads to the center."* —Christina Baldwin

23

When someone we love dies and we feel suffering, it does not mean that something is wrong. Going into the wilderness of the soul with other human beings is anchored in walking with them through spiritual distress without thinking we have to have them attain "resolution" or "recovery."

Being in the wilderness relates to being in liminal space. *Limina* is the Latin word for threshold, the space betwixt and between. Liminal space is that spiritual place where most people hate to be, but where the experience of grief leads them. This is often where the griever's worldview—the set of beliefs about how the world functions and what place they as individuals occupy therein—comes into question. Putting one's shattered worldview back together paradoxically requires companions who do not think their helping role is to fix or give answers or explanations. There is no technique, no formula, no prescription for the wilderness experience.

A critical part of being present to someone in the wilderness of the soul is to be open to states of not knowing the outcome or trying to force the outcome. Most North Americans have trouble trusting in this process and feel an instinctive need to get the mourner out of the wilderness, or, at the very least, try to move her to the left or the right. We have become a people who demand answers and explanations and expect fast and efficient resolutions.

## The Ambiguity of Loss

We don't like pain, sadness, anxiety, ambiguity, loss of control—all normal symptoms of the wilderness of grief. We want to experience light before we encounter darkness. If we as caregivers cannot be still in the presence of these care-eliciting symptoms, we will be tempted to explain or treat them away. After all, we falsely think that any explanation is better than being in liminal space. A sense of control is better than the terrible "cloud of unknowing." Yet, the opposite of control is actually participation—in this context, participation in the work of mourning while one is "under reconstruction."

The challenge for many caregivers is to stay on the threshold of the wilderness without consciously or unconsciously demanding or projecting a desire for resolution. In other words, there is a tendency to be attached to outcome, not open to outcome. Obviously, the instinct to move the mourner away from pain and suffering is rooted in the desire to stay distant from one's own pain.

Sadly, many people, caregivers and lay public alike, have come to regard grief as an enemy. Brokenness is not something we choose to invite in. Instead of honoring the wise words of Joseph Addison, who once said, "I will indulge my sorrows, and give way to all the pangs and fury of despair," our contemporary mantra seems to be more aligned with the words of the Bobby McFerrin song: "Don't Worry, Be Happy!"

**Under Reconstruction**
To be bereaved literally means "to be torn apart." When someone has been torn apart by grief, they are in essence "under reconstruction." Maslow's famous hierarchy of human needs teaches us that our most fundamental needs—for shelter, food, water, sleep—must first be met before we can meet our higher-order needs. Thus the mourner's physical needs must be taken care of, followed, in Maslow's order, by his needs for safety, love/belonging, esteem, and actualization. To heal, he must reconstruct his entire life from the ground up.

## The No Place That is Grief

In contrast, ancient cultures seemed to understand the value of being in the wilderness as a part of any kind of major transition in life's journey. They often invited themselves into the wilderness through experiences such as spending 40 days in the desert, climbing to the mountaintops, and taking solo journeys into the ocean. Whatever the underlying set of beliefs, to get where he was eventually going, the journeyer first had to experience going to nowhere, to release himself from who and what he

*"The clearest way into the universe is through a forest wilderness."*—John Muir

had been. In the "no place" of the wilderness, he could begin building a new person and place again.

This resonates with my experience of companioning people in life transitions. It seems we cannot integrate loss into our lives until we embrace the fear and sometimes raw terror of going to this "no place" wilderness and descending into it on our way through it. Then and only then do we begin to notice that something begins to slowly shift as we open our hearts to the pain of grief.

Of course, there are powerful forces that invite mourners to do otherwise. We are told to "keep busy," "carry on," and "find someone to meet." Following these mourning-avoidant scripts, the griever may try to retrace her steps back to a time or place that feels familiar, a place to find one's "old self"—but that old self is gone forever. Now, being temporarily lost in the wilderness of grief *is* the familiar place. Slowly, over time and with gentle companions, the mourner can search for renewed meaning and discover a new self.

But through this time of turmoil, the discomfort and mystery of being in the wilderness are meant to be. In reality, it is actually a kind of "purification phase"—just one phase of the journey that will very slowly change into something else. The important thing is to learn to honor and respect this process and to lean into it despite the instinct to do otherwise.

No, it is not comfortable to be betwixt and between—to be helpless, out of control, depressed, anxious, and to not know. Again, if we look to other cultures we discover that in parts of Africa, a person who is in a place of not knowing is considered to be in a place of "walking the land of gray clouds." During times of uncertainty and not knowing, it is considered inappropriate, even foolish, to take action. In fact, it is considered an act of wisdom to wait and trust the process. The opposite of trusting the process is trying to control the uncontrollable—obviously an impossible task when it involves experiences of grief and mourning.

## Detachment and Grief

Central to not being attached
to outcome is the concept of
detachment. The majority of
Westerners think of "detachment"
as a lack of warmth and caring. Yet,
linguistically, the word detachment
is often defined as "the capacity
to come deeply from an objective
place." Considered from this
perspective, detachment can be seen

as not trying to control what you can't control. In part, it is
"going with the symptom." It is observing what the soul is
teaching about the depth of feeling and not trying to change
it. You stay present to what is without thinking you need to
change it or take it away. You observe the soul; you don't mask
or try to do away with symptoms of soul work. All this time,
you stay patient and recognize that going through grief is more
necessary than going around it or moving beyond it.

When you are detached, you are still very much present to
the deep soul work that is taking place. This is about not

getting pulled into feeling responsible for taking away the pain of the loss. Actually, you care deeply in a way that allows you to be totally present to what is there rather than what you wish was there. You could consider this a homeopathic response of going with what is presented as opposed to against it. You are open to outcome, not attached to outcome! Or, as the Zen statement observes in a lovely way, "Spring comes, and the grass grows all by itself." The companion is able to acknowledge that less effort is sometimes better.

**Divine Momentum**
In grief, Divine Momentum is the notion that the process of mourning will, all by itself, lead to healing and reconciliation. In embracing and expressing their grief, mourners will, over time and with the support of others, move forward. To trust in Divine Momentum is to believe that healing can and will unfold. As a companion, you help create Divine Momentum for healing by offering a safe starting place for the journey. You offer a free and open space for mourners to give attention to that which they need to give attention to.

## New Models of Grief Care

This orientation to caring is in contrast to modern psychological approaches that tend toward a more rational and logical understanding of matters of the heart. Modern psychology invites people to identify a problem and fix it. "Managed care" is just that—managed care. Very few models exist wherein we see the value of soul and symptoms of distress that need to be reflected on, observed, and respected.

We need soul-based models of caring that demonstrate the sensitivity of the heart. We need models that allow mourners to stay open to the mystery as they encounter the wilderness of their grief. We need models that respect that we don't have to understand and control everything that surrounds us. In fact, perhaps it is in "standing under" the mysterious experience of death that provides us with a unique perspective. We are not above or bigger than death. Maybe only after discovering the liminal space of the wilderness, in which we do not "understand," can we patiently discover renewed meaning and purpose in our continued living.

## Surrendering to Grief

In my experience, "understanding" comes when we as companions help grievers surrender: surrender any need to compare their grief (it's not a competition); surrender any self-critical judgments (self-compassion is a critical ingredient to integrating loss into life); and surrender any need to completely understand (we never do because mystery is something to be pondered, not explained).

The grief that touches our souls has its own voice and should not be compromised by a need for comparison, judgment, or even complete understanding. Actually, surrendering to the unknowable wilderness of grief is a courageous choice, an act of faith, a trust in God and in oneself. The grieving person can only hold this mystery in her heart and surround herself with compassionate, non-judgmental companions. My hope is that is YOU—the reader of this book.

For transformation of grief to unfold, you have to surrender to the experience. Trying to stay in control by denying, inhibiting, or converting grief can result in what Kierkegaard termed "unconscious despair." Doing the soul work of grief

*"There sometimes seems to be an inverse relationship between information and wisdom... We have many demanding academic programs in professional psychology, and states often have rigid requirements for the practice of psychotherapy, and yet there is undoubtedly a severe dearth of wisdom about the mysteries of the soul."*
—Thomas Moore

demands going into and through suffering and integrating it in ways that help unite you with your fellow strugglers and the greater community of people.

John Keats observed in Shakespeare what he called a "negative capability"…"the capacity to be in mystery and doubt without any irritable searching after fact and reason." I have discovered that one way to survive the wilderness experience is to remember that you are doing the hard work of mourning even when you may seem to be doing nothing. And even when the mourner feels like he is making the slowest of progress and edging out of the deep wilderness, there will be times when he will feel like he is backtracking and being ravaged by the forces around him. This, too, is the nature of grief. Complete mastery of a wilderness experience is not possible. Just as we cannot control the winds and storms and the beasts in nature, we can never have total dominion over our grief. However, as the griever experiences the wilderness, he both needs and deserves caring companions along the way.

# Tenet Three

## Companioning is about honoring the spirit;
## it is not about focusing on the intellect.

*"The ultimate cure, as many ancient and modern psychologies of depth have asserted, comes from love and not from logic."* —Thomas Moore

To be torn apart and to then become whole again, we need more than our intellect. We need the experiences that spring from the spirit and the soul. "Spirit" can be broadly defined as our nonphysical essences, which include dimensions of intellect, emotion, personality, and spirituality. I often perceive the spirit as the "life-force." As human beings, we are spirit explorers who have stepped into bodies here on earth.

"Soul" is not a thing but a quality or dimension of experiencing life. Thomas Moore notes that soul "has to do with depth, value, relatedness, heart, and personal substance." If you wish to companion people in grief, I believe you must be present to matters of the spirit and soul.

Obviously, we as humans seek protection from raw emotions by, at times, intellectualizing the experiences of grief. We move back and forth between head and heart, between intellect and feeling. I submit that in contemporary North America, we are often invited to think around losses instead of feel them through. We bring to grief a fix-it attitude, assuming that the experience is something to be overcome and that you would be well served to "let go" of it and move on quickly and efficiently.

Yet, matters of the spirit and soul are not made for letting go and moving on in some perfectionist, intellectual fashion. If we want to give attention to the spirit and the soul, then we have to discard the "resolution wish" and give care in ways that respect the energy of grief. As John Donne, the poet of relationship and soul, once observed, "He who has no time to mourn, has no time to mend." Respect for grief demands our appreciation for its complexity.

## Accepting What Is

When we look at the spirit and soul of grief, we discover value in slowing down and not trying to take away

> "All suffering prepares the soul for vision."
> —Martin Buber

painful emotions that are a necessary part of the journey. If we join the griever in only trying to think through loss, we are trying to avoid the reaches of the spirit and the soul. When you as a caregiver give attention to the messages from the spirit and soul, you empathize with the uncomfortable thoughts and feelings that are inherent to the journey.

Working within this premise encourages you to support the grieving person in taking back what she is often trying to intellectually disown, such as depression, anxiety, and loss of control. As opposed to wishing they weren't there, you work with the raw emotions by entering into them. Instead of trying to manage the grief the person is experiencing, you realize the value of the grief managing the person. As the Greek philosopher Heraclitus observed many years ago, "The soul has its own source of unfolding."

A homeopathic response to grief is to go with what is presented rather than against it. We befriend grief instead of making an enemy of it. Instead of trying to quickly get away from our grief, we savor it.

If the griever is experiencing deep sadness, then the spirit and soul are expressing the rhythms of the journey into and through grief. Instead of trying to outmaneuver these forces and use some premature technique to return life to "normal" (an inappropriate helping goal), I submit that the more authentic way of being in tune with the soul is in the direction of the symptoms. Any other response is like fighting with what the spirit and soul are bringing forth.

Have you noticed how depression has gotten a bad name these days? It's like we expect we have some God-given right to never be depressed. Yet, in my experience, normal life circumstances, such as the death of someone precious to us, can naturally result in depression, particularly if defined in the following way:

*Depression*: A turning inward when the world outside no longer seems to be charged with meaning and purpose.

## Respecting the Work of the Soul

I find that as a companion who tries to be respectful of soul and spirit work, my role is to empathize with what is being expressed in the moment. For example, if a person comes into my Center for Loss and says, "I can't get my feet out of bed in the morning," my responsibility is not to use some technique to help this person overcome the lethargy of grief accompanied by profound sadness. Instead, my role is to empathize with what it is like to be a lost spirit and soul. I try to help the mourner embrace her soul work. The mourner often projects, directly or indirectly, "Someone precious has died. I feel so alone right now. My body, spirit, and soul are depressed. I lack meaning and purpose in my daily life right now. What am I trying to experience so that slowly, over time, I can discover renewed meaning in my life?" This kind of communication for the mourner demands an empathetic responsiveness that helps

39

create a non-judgmental companioning relationship with this person.

Being respectful might lead me to simply respond in ways that encourage her to be self-compassionate about the normalcy of the physical and emotional symptoms of her grief. I might restate for her, "So, right now, it's hard to get your feet out of bed." My response to people in grief is based on the belief that the only way beyond the experience of grief is through the experience of grief. The mourner must descend before she can transcend. Many contemporary "therapies" get this descend–transcend experience out of order.

Yes, when the spirit and soul come to life in grief, the ordinary wisdom or intellectual life loses much of its power. To avoid our own pain, we may be tempted to offer up some rational advice like, "Being depressed isn't going to bring the person who died back." Yet, these kind of rationalizations are not helpful in the end. Repression of the voices of the spirit and soul only serve to move the griever farther away from the ultimate integration of the death into her life. Even depression has the capacity to propel the mourner to insights that can result in eventual renewal.

Honoring the spirit and soul is about being honest about the sting of grief and acknowledging the reality of the depth of the loss. Some native cultures describe "speaking with spirit tongue" when they emphasize the importance of being

*"Do you not see how necessary a world of pains and troubles is to school an intelligence and make it a soul?"* —John Keats

*"I never came upon any of my discoveries through the process of rational thinking."* —Albert Einstein

honest and telling the truth. Honoring the spirit and soul is what I refer to as "listening with the spirit ear," wherein you witness the honest pain of the loss and affirm the need of the mourner to tell the truth about the transformational journey of grief.

In reflecting on the vital importance of honoring the spirit and soul of grief, I think about the shamanic concept of sacred hoops, which is synonymous with the term "authenticity" or being connected to your own spirituality. The idea is that when you experience being yourself, you are in your sacred hoop, and when you are being genuinely who you are without pretense, you are sitting inside your sacred hoop. Being truly who you are when companioning people in grief allows you to honor the spirit—the life force—of another human being.

A soul- and spirit-centered understanding of grief mandates a different language from that of traditional mental health care. We companion our fellow strugglers by honoring their expressions of grief, recognizing that spirit and soul have their own purposes, and supporting them more from our hearts than from our heads.

# Tenet Four

Companioning is about listening with the heart; it is not about analyzing with the head.

*"Listen and attend with the ear of your heart."* —Saint Benedict

Scientific analyses about grief and therapeutic theories surrounding interventions often result in caregivers

> *"The heart holds answers the brain refuses to see."* —Robert Kall

overlooking the sacred art of listening with the heart. In fact, there are a multitude of invitations to use your head to assess, diagnose, and treat, which, by default, encourage you to stay distant from the heart.

Our language is replete with references to the heart that give testimony to our instinctual understanding of this part of our divinity and humanity: "Take heart;" "the heart of the matter;" and "home is where the heart is" are but a few of a multitude of references to the heart in our everyday conversations. We know deeply that authentic mourning is a quest for the healing of our broken hearts.

My years of learning from my own losses—as well as the losses of those who have trusted me to walk with them—have taught me that the path of the heart applies to both the mourner and the companion. Listening with the heart is anchored in the capacity to express compassion and understanding and to possess a deep desire to show solidarity with people experiencing grief. Nowhere are we hungrier for more heart-based, soul-centered models than in the area of grief care.

## The Power of Open-Heartedness

The good news is that as companions we can do just that—minister to people in grief from a place of open-heartedness. However, you will have to remember to be a responsible rebel—to question assumptions, to work from this attitude. Why? Because like me, probably

> *"Listening is an attitude of the heart, a genuine desire to be with another which both attracts and heals."* —J. Isham

no one in your schooling told you, "Listen with your heart. Minister to others from a place of open-heartedness." So, as I did, you may have to learn this on your own or seek out other responsible rebels as mentors.

I do believe we can set our intention toward being open-hearted and then make the time and effort to bring it about. First comes the internal decision: I will work from a place of open-heartedness. There are so many forces working against this today (e.g., managed care, brief therapies, evidence-based practices, a fast-paced culture, a lack of understanding of the role of hurt in healing) that it will not happen without that internal decision. In addition, the internal decision will likely have to be based on something that has genuine meaning to you: feeling nudged that this is the way to be present to your fellow human beings; being inspired by hearing someone talk about this way of being; or an innate desire that has always been a part of who you are.

In our search for ministry from a place of open-heartedness, I reflect on the importance of four critical ingredients: humility; unknowing; unconditional love; and what I have come to call a spiritual practice of "readiness to receive" a fellow human being. Allow me to explore each one of these with you.

## Humility

Humility is grounded in realizing you are not an expert about grief. You are the student who is being taught by the true expert—the person in grief. Humility is also about a willingness to learn from your mistakes as well as an appreciation of your limitations and strengths. When you come from a place of humility, your

*"Wear your learning like your watch, in a private pocket; and do not pull it out, and strike it, merely to show that you have one."* —Lord Chesterfield

46

behavior is welcoming, tolerant, and nonjudgmental. You come from a place of the open soul that is totally present, compassionate, and peace-filled.

## Unknowing

Unknowing means being completely present to the mourner with an open mind and an open heart. This does not mean an absence of thought, but, in contrast, a very clear attentiveness to the moment. Unknowing is not achieved by some conscious effort or technique but by letting go—giving up any need to be in control or manage someone's grief journey. Unknowing guides our hearts to the path of our soul and creates a safe space for the griever to authentically mourn. The domain of the soul is where one can encounter what is most feared and open to what it might be tempting to close oneself off from. When we initiate helping from a place of unknowing, the full measure of our soul is available to reach out in support of those in grief.

## Unconditional Love and Acceptance

The very essence of open-heartedness is the capacity to express unconditional love and acceptance of the mourner.

Just as love is at the center of grief, love is also the core of compassionate caregiving. Unconditional love is the expression of the Divine flowing through you with no expectations attached.

Unconditional love creates a sacred safe space for the griever to authentically mourn. At the same time, this kind of love creates a sense of personal responsibility in the mourner. As a companion, you are responsible *to* the mourner, not *for* the mourner. Part of the paradox of communicating unconditional love is that it frees the mourner to do her work instead of you thinking it is something you do for her. Unconditional love creates a safe harbor in which to mourn, but it does not overprotect or hinder the freedom to mourn.

Unconditional love elevates your caregiving to the transpersonal realm of experience. Our open hearts are able to become pathways through which Divine

*"Give love and unconditional acceptance to those you encounter and notice what happens."* —Wayne Dyer

love is expressed to the mourner. The companion relationship becomes sacred as it basks in the wisdom and healing powers of unconditional love.

## Understanding the Five Levels of Unconditional Love

**Physical level:** You feel a sense of lightness, a sense of warmth and caring that is felt in the throat and chest area, particularly the area of the heart; you feel relaxed and honored to be in the presence of someone willing to allow you to honor her grief journey.

**Cognitive level:** You are nonjudgmental and accepting of how the mourner may think differently about her grief experience than you do; you do not assess or diagnose; you "seek to understand" without judgment; you are welcoming and tolerant.

**Emotional level:** You feel open and present to a full spectrum of emotions, whatever they might be; you are committed to consciously exploring how your own emotions are impacted as you companion your fellow human beings; you feel emotionally congruent in your helping role and may well recognize you have found your calling.

**Social level:** You recognize that your capacity to create a "sacred, safe space" to give attention to another's grief is at the center of the definition of mourning: "the shared social response to loss"; you are humbled that people are willing to make use of your personhood in this way; you are happy to be the companion you are; you feel your heart is at home in this helping role.

**Spiritual level:** You convey a sense of gentle, positive, creative energy anchored in compassion, meaning a willingness "to suffer with"; you have a desire to give to others and "walk with" or "break bread" with them; you realize you touch at the soul level when you reach out with your heart instead of your mind; you feel a trust and optimism surrounding the mourner's capacity to bring forth grief in ways that lead to healing and wholeness.

Matthew Fox, theologian and educator, wisely observed, "When we are joyous and full of heart, we are emanating wisdom. Wisdom is not in the head but in the heart and gut where compassion is felt." Unconditional love is expressed through the five transpersonal levels introduced above. Once you have the courage to minister to those in grief from a place of love instead of clinical distance, you will discover your inherent passion to be a companion.

Unconditional love puts you into a "flow-like" state of being. When you are in this flow experience, you are externally focused on the moment-to-moment needs of the mourner. The mourner can actually feel and experience your heartfelt compassion. To achieve flow, you must consciously cultivate your capacity to actively express love that is revealed at the soul level.

Unconditional love is experienced and expressed on all five levels of our being: physical, cognitive, emotional, social, and spiritual. When you become committed to expressing your life energy in these five levels, you will radiate the gift and grace of unconditional love. Then you can truly be the companion you were meant to be.

## Readiness to Receive

Over the years I have discovered the value of a spiritual practice I use to prepare my heart and soul to be present to mourners in ways that facilitate the expression of humility, unknowing, and unconditional love. I have come to refer to this practice as my "readiness to receive" ritual.

Just before I see anyone for support in their journey, I center myself in a quiet place, inside or outside the Center for Loss and Life Transition. By creating a sacred space and stepping away from the business of the day, I seek to find quietness and stillness. In a very real sense I'm preparing my soul to be totally present to the grieving person or family. This practice is a way of letting go of anything that might get in the way of my open-heartedness. I seem to need this time to listen to myself before I can listen to others.

Once I have gone quiet, I repeat a three-phrase mantra to myself. The three phrases are:

"No rewards for speed"

"Divine Momentum"

"Not attached to outcome"

These words help me slow down, recognize my role is to help create momentum for the griever to authentically mourn life losses, and always remember the vital importance of being present to people where they are instead of where I might think they need to be. After repeating these phrases for two to three minutes, I usually conclude with some kind of affirmation like, "I thank the universe for providing me the opportunity to help people mourn well so they can go on to live well and love well."

Obviously, your spiritual practice of readiness to receive a fellow human being may be different than mine. Yet, I do hope you consider some ritual that propels you to a place of open-heartedness. Yes, your open heart is a well of reception; it will be moved entirely by what it perceives. Then a beautiful process unfolds: Listening and responding from the heart, you are patiently empathetic to the needs of the mourner. She then begins to sense your belief, and, more important, her own belief, in her capacity to integrate the death of someone precious into her life. You are honored and privileged to be a small part of this journey.

# Tenet Five

## Companioning is about bearing witness to the struggles of others; it is not about judging or directing these struggles.

*"Too often we underestimate the power of a touch, a smile, a kind word, a listening ear, an honest compliment, or the smallest act of caring, all of which have the potential to turn a life around."* —Leo Buscaglia

Bearing witness to the struggles of someone experiencing the darkness of grief—having empathy—is the deepest form of emotional and spiritual interaction you can have with another human being. If you can hear another person's words of pain and loss, not from a place of clinical distance but from a place of an open heart, then you can bring a

> *"Some people think only intellect counts: knowing how to solve problems, knowing how to get by, knowing how to identify an advantage and seize it. But the functions of intellect are insufficient without courage, love, friendship, compassion, and empathy."*
> —Dean Koontz

fully alive human presence to bear on the other human being's experiences. Overcoming any tendency to judge will allow you to be taught by the griever. This active empathy will naturally create an environment in which healing can and will occur.

Entering into and bearing witness to the anguish of raw grief can be overwhelming, for to actually be able to enter into another person's experience so completely that she is able to feel your companionship is the embodiment of the highest degree of emotional and spiritual refinement. To truly join the mourner in the place of her helplessness requires that we as caregivers visit our own griefs and experience our transformed hearts.

## Doing Your Own Work First

The supporting cradle of empathy evolves from the collage of feelings we have come to encounter in our own personal journeys into grief. You may find that if you haven't felt a particular feeling, or if you are unwilling or unable to reencounter it, your capacity to be present to another person will be inhibited. You may even see the loss as something that has happened to "her" and not to "you" and thus lose your openness, your compassionate presence. Your empathy with her struggles will be a feeble attempt at embracing the feelings, not a truly empathetic experience.

*"The heart that breaks open can contain the whole universe."*
—Joanna Macy

*"Compassion is the basis of morality."*
—Arnold Schopenhauer

That is why bearing witness to the struggles of those in grief is such a demanding ministry. You have to do your own work first to acquaint yourself in depth with your soul-based emotions. Only then, because you have authentically felt, will you "know what it feels like." You will have an anchor in your own soul for what a grief experience may feel like to a fellow human being. Since you have been there, you can enter into struggles such as discovering a reason to go on living,

55

redefining one's worldview, and searching for meaning in life and living.

A natural inhibition in the willingness to enter into the wilderness of grief is that we are often hesitant, or literally afraid, of reopening our own wounds. Instead of being able to companion a fellow struggler, we may be overwhelmed by the conscious recreation of our own painful feelings. So, instead of being open to the presence of the pain of the loss, we may deny people their experiences ("It could be worse"); we may problem-solve or technique people ("Here's what to do so you can let go"); or we may minimize or compare experiences ("You think you have it bad? Let me tell you what happened to someone else").

To be able to enter into the wilderness with a person in the depths of grief, therefore, requires the embracing of our own heartfelt emotions, not in the sense of mastering them, but in allowing them to flow through us. Then, and only then, are we able to give the most precious gift—our compassionate companionship.

## Expressing Compassion

Bearing witness to the struggles of people in grief is about having compassion. Compassion is from the words *cum pation*, meaning "to suffer with," "to undergo with," "to share solidarity with." Compassion

embraces our common humanity, our feelings of togetherness, our experiences of kinship. This word compassion has been so much in exile in the mainstream grief counseling literature, yet it is the very essence of what bereaved people both need and deserve. Therefore, the theme of this book is about healing grief as a philosophical and literal act of removing the obstacles to compassion. While empathy refers to "feeling with" the grieving person, compassion is about "feeling for" the grieving person. You have to care for and about the person to be a soulful companion.

Actively expressing compassion through bearing witness to the struggles of others is by no means elitist. Anyone and everyone can express compassion to someone encountering grief. You don't have to have a college degree to express compassion. You don't have to be a certified grief counselor to express compassion. You only need to have a heart full of grace and a soul anchored in love.

## Bearing Witness Means Being Involved in the Feeling World

Bearing witness to the struggles of the griever is anchored in striving to understand the meaning of her experience from the inside out rather than imposing meaning on the experience from the outside in. Active empathy means the caregiver is attentively involved in a process of exploration. The companion is trying to grasp what it is like inside the soul—the life force—of the griever.

Empathetic responsiveness requires the ability to go beyond the surface and to become involved in the mourner's feeling world, but always with an "as if" quality of taking another's role without personally experiencing what the other person experiences. What is the inner flavor and what are the unique meanings that the person's experience has for him? What is it that she is trying to express but can't quite say in words?

This empathetic, "bearing witness" process is in contrast to both sympathy and identification. Sympathy is a feeling of concern for someone else without necessarily becoming involved in a close, helping relationship; it projects an "I feel sorry for you" attitude, but stops short of empathy. More destructive than sympathy is identification. This attitude is conveyed by those who submerge themselves with the griever and try to take on their feelings for them. These are people who make assumptions like, "I know just how you feel." The last person the griever feels safe with are those who convey this attitude of over-identification.

*"Witness the contents of mind, the visions and sounds, the thoughts, as clouds passing through the vast expanse— the sky-like nature of mind. The rootedness of Being is in emptiness, clarity and awareness: unborn, unspoilt, stainlessly pure."* —Alex Grey

## Bearing Witness Means Going Beyond "I Know How You Feel"

Bearing witness from a place of active empathy is experienced when the mourner feels you understand. To simply say, "I understand how you feel" is not enough. Empathy is communicated when you, the companion, respond at the emotional, feeling level of the mourner. You reach the mourner where he is, being careful not to bring judgment or a need to get him to "let go" and "move on." This dependable quality of empathy is what seems to free the mourner to open his heart and mourn from the inside out.

## Bearing Witness Means Not Trying to "Fix Things"

The more you encourage the mourner to teach you from a position of concerned curiosity, the less you will feel any need to "fix things." As you allow yourself to be taught, you are relieved of any burden to get people where you would like them to go. In other words, you are not attached to outcome.

The paradoxical aspect of this attitude is that the more you allow yourself to be taught and follow the mourner's lead, the more integration of the loss seems to take place. At least this is a very real part of my experience and probably one of the greatest gifts I have discovered in my life's work.

## Bearing Witness Means Embracing Feelings of Loss

Observation suggests that some people who attempt to help grieving people hesitate to elicit and embrace feelings such as sadness, loneliness, anxiety, and hurt, often fearing that the expression of these feelings at the least "won't do any good," or, at most, will "make matters worse." However, experience suggests that such hesitation is a form of defensive protection for the caregiver who finds it threatening to respond at any true emotional-spiritual level to the mourner.

Just because feelings are threatening does not mean that we as companions should avoid encouraging their expression in the mourner. We should never avoid what a mourner feels because we fear she cannot take it. She is always taking it. The question is whether you will support her in experiencing it with your compassionate presence or only in the isolation of being alone with it. We could also reframe this to note: We as caregivers should never avoid what a mourner implicitly feels because we fear *we* cannot take it!

## Benefits of Bearing Witness Without Bringing Judgment

The capacity to convey active empathy while bearing witness has a number of benefits for the mourner. Among them are the following:

• Empathetic communication is a foundation upon which you establish a companion-witness relationship with the mourner.

• The mourner who feels empathetically understood and not judged is more likely to risk sharing deep, soul-based encounters with grief.

• The mourner's experience of your genuine effort and commitment to understand creates a trusting, low-threat environment that negates the need for self-protection and isolation.

• The communication of empathy encourages self-exploration in the mourner, a prerequisite for compassionate self-understanding and, eventually, movement (with "no rewards for speed") toward reconciliation.

Our choices about attitude related to how to support our fellow human beings in grief often seem to relate to motives and needs. Adopting a bearing-witness-to-the-struggles attitude of "teach me about your grief and I will be with you without judgment" means we give up the status that sometimes falsely comes from being a professional "expert." However, I suspect that in giving up or letting go of some of this ego-based identity, we may well discover our natural compassion.

# Tenet Six

## Companioning is about walking alongside;
## it is not about leading.

*"The most familiar models of who we are—doctor and patient, 'helper' and 'helped'—often turn out to be major obstacles to the expression of our caring instincts; they limit the full measure of what we have to offer one another... True compassion arises out of unity."* —Ram Dass

I truly believe that the largest impediment to providing compassionate support to grieving people is the professional distinction we often make between "us" and "them." Invested in models of separateness, we end up creating distance in the helping relationship. The more you see yourself as having superior knowledge of someone else's grief experience, the more need there is for the griever to play the passive role of being helped.

In my ministry in grief care, I've discovered that true healing lies within the mourner, not the "expert counselor." True compassion evolves when you, the companion, see yourself as a fellow traveler, not as an expert in the mourner's journey. The more you can walk alongside and learn from the mourner, the more you will experience the true grace of an equal relationship of unity.

Another way to think of yourself is as a holder of mirrors. You, as grief companion, never really "heal" anyone. Instead, you help people heal themselves by holding up mirrors. As they peer into the mirrors, mourners may experience a shift, a transformation of experience anchored in the heart and the soul.

This tenet describes those qualities that I have discovered allow the companion to walk alongside the grieving person. Artful companions are those who keep their hearts open wide and always continue to learn from the true expert—the mourner. If by some chance your heart has closed off, perhaps the discussion that follows will help you soften and re-open your heart.

This tenet begs the question, "How can we establish a relationship with the mourner that provides a safe environment wherein she feels free to authentically express grief without fear of judgment, isolation, or abandonment?" What follows is a brief introduction to the qualities that allow you to walk alongside the mourner. For a separate discussion of the core quality of empathy, see Tenet Five.

## Respect

This important quality relates to a nonpossessive caring for and affirmation of the mourner as a separate person capable of healing from the inside out. Respect involves a receptive attitude of having the mourner teach you about her experience of grief. The opposite of this respectful companioning partnership would be the caregiver who presumptuously believes that her superior knowledge of grief qualifies her to project what is best for the mourner to think, feel, and do.

## Sensitivity and Warmth

Sensitivity and warmth in the companion are demonstrated through a sense of personal closeness to the mourner as opposed to professional distance. Distancing themselves from their own or another's pain and acting like they are experts are ways some caregivers get into trouble. Some counselors are even trained to stay professionally distant and come across as cold and impersonal. There is such truth in the saying, "People don't care about how much you know until they know how much you care." Above all, sensitivity and warmth imply patience and the capacity to respond in a nonjudgmental way to the needs of the mourner.

## Genuineness

The companion must be truly herself—non-phony and non-defensive. Your words and actions should match your inner feelings. Genuineness results in interpersonal richness. When the mourner senses you are genuine, she can authentically express what is on her heart.

## Trust

Trust is about consistency and safety. Grieving people often naturally feel a lack of trust in the world because of the death of someone loved. They sometimes wonder if they should risk trusting or loving again. As a companion, you have an obligation to help the mourner feel consistently safe with you. When trust happens between two people, there is a noticeable exchange of energy. And conversely, when trust is lacking or absent, no energy is exchanged and nothing happens.

## Immediacy

This quality has to do with being present to the mourner in the here and now. It goes beyond the content of what is being said to the process of what is happening from moment to moment. The high-functioning companion has the gift of high levels of immediacy. The mourner's needs are right there in the present moment, and immediacy allows you to be empathetically responsive to those needs. The present moment is where the needs of the soul reside—and grief work is anchored in soul work.

# Humility

This connotes a willingness to learn from one's own mistakes as well as an appreciation of one's limitations and strengths. Humility also means continually being aware of how your own experiences with loss are impacting your presence to the mourner. Helpers who are humble remember to ask questions of themselves such as, "How am I being impacted by sharing in the mourner's experience with grief?"; "Does the mourner's experience with loss remind me of some of my own losses?"; "Where can I share the feelings that supporting this mourner stimulates in me?" Humility means you are not the expert but are open to learning what each new companioning relationship has to teach you about being helpful at this moment in time. And humility interfaces with developing a service ethic— genuinely wanting to care for others, while at the same time realizing you are not "in charge." Instead, you submit yourself to the tenets of companioning (as opposed to treating) and open your soul to the mysterious journey called grief.

## Patience

To be patient with the mourner is to let him mourn in his own way and time at a pace he is comfortable with. Some of the deepest communication you may have with a grieving person comes during times of silence and solitude. Being patient is a means of building trust and enhancing the mourner's awareness that you are there to bear witness and learn from his unique experiences. Patience is a very quiet, unassuming quality—the capacity to wait for what is unseen and unspoken to be gradually made manifest. Patience also denotes a quietness of spirit, a deep inner knowing that you will stay present and stand at the mourner's side.

## Hope

I believe it is impossible to be a true companion without this quality, for it is in having hope that you communicate your belief that the mourner can and will heal, or "become whole again."

Hope is an expectation of a good that is yet to be. It is an expression of the present alive with a sense of the possible. You create hope in the mourner by having hope in your heart and providing acceptance, recognition, affirmation, and gratitude in the context of your helping relationship. Hope rallies energies and activates the courage to the commitment of mourning.

## Humor

Even in the midst of grief, moments of humor spontaneously occur. How much lighter we feel when we laugh in the midst of our pain. Too much sitting in seriousness violates the laws of the universe.

## Heart

To have "heart" as you companion people in grief is to be true to your own feelings, humanness, and vulnerabilities. When you work from a place of heart, you function as a whole. When your analytical, thinking self is in charge, you may be just in your head. Yet, the centerpiece of the integration of grief is not the mind, but the heart. Being a companion naturally occurs when you relax into yourself and bring compassion to all of your helping efforts.

This allows you to fulfill not only your personal passion to help those in grief, but also your highest purpose that will be part of your contribution to helping all people mourn well so they can go on to live well and love well. When you minister from the heart, you are in a state of deep connection with the divine, with yourself, and with other human beings. You do not minister alone, but in the companionship of other companions.

Once you have explored the ten qualities outlined in this chapter, considering your strengths and weaknesses, it is probably best to forget all this and return to this tenet only when you feel that one or more of these qualities is missing in your helping relationships. When you feel yourself struggling in a companioning relationship, you may find that it is because you have temporarily lost touch with one or more of these qualities.

# Tenet Seven

Companioning is about discovering the gifts of sacred silence; it does not mean filling up every moment with words.

*"Do not speak unless you can improve upon silence."* —Buddhist teaching

In discovering the gifts of sacred silence, you cultivate what becomes an avenue for the mourner to open his heart up to wisdom surrounding the grief journey. As you quiet yourself, you sustain an open heart and a gentle spirit.

As you focus your every attention on the mourner, you are a source of nourishment. As you companion one person at a time, your compassionate concentration helps quiet the many other potential contenders for your undivided attention.

## The Gift of Silence

*"Silence is not absence of sound but rather a shifting of attention toward wounds that speak to the soul."*
—Thomas Moore

The mystery of grief has taught me that it requires periods of solitude and silence. The griever may not have access to a cloistered monastery, a walk in the woods, or a stroll on the beach. But, she does have access to your quiet presence and loving spirit. Consciously hush yourself and place trust in the

*"Non-judgment creates silence of the mind."*
—Deepak Chopra

peace you help initiate. Become fully present to another human being who doesn't really need your words but values your soulful presence.

76

Being silently present to someone in grief requires discernment as to where you channel your energy, your care, your compassion. As you sit with silence, you acknowledge that you value the need to suspend, slow down, and turn inward as part of the grief journey. Giving honor to the instinct to mourn from the inside out requires that we as caregivers come to cherish silence and respect how vital it is to the healing journey.

Silence also asks that we respect the role of hurt and pain in healing. If we do not understand this, we will not be capable of silencing our tongues. Instead, we will feel the urge to speak, thinking consciously or unconsciously that we must fix the griever. In so doing, we get in the way of the needed space to initiate the mending of a broken heart. What a gift to come to know the healing power of silence!

## Grief Symptoms and Silence

I find it enlightening to explore how it is that many of the symptoms of grief are invitations to the need for silence and solitude. Perhaps the most isolating and frightening part of grief for many people is the sense of disorganization, confusion, searching, and yearning that often comes with the loss. As one person noted, "I felt as if I were a lonely traveler with no companion and worse yet, no destination. I could not find myself or anybody else." Yes, the mourner needs silence and solitude.

Another common symptom of grief is the onset of poor judgment-making capabilities. Good judgment is grounded in making choices that are in the best interest of yourself and those for whom you are responsible. Many mourners temporarily lose the capability to make sound judgments. Yes, the mourner needs silence and solitude.

Another common symptom is loss of perspective and a search for meaning. Life naturally seems darker right now than it did otherwise. Life feels distorted, out of perspective. There are sometimes a multitude of

*"Why did God give man two ears and one mouth? So that he will hear more and talk less."*
—Adapted from the Hasdai

*"For many afflictions, silence is the best remedy."* —Talmud

"why" questions to which there are no quick answers. "Why did the person I love have to die now?" "Why should I go on living?" Yes, the mourner needs silence and solitude.

Yet another symptom is the lethargy of grief. Fatigue tries to slow the mourner down and invites a need for privacy. The lethargy that accompanies grief is often more than simply being tired. It reflects that the body's immune system is depleted and that the griever has lost the energy and capacity to respond. The body has such wisdom. Yes, the mourner needs silence and solitude.

The companionship of silence has the ingredients that can bring some peace in the midst of the wilderness. The forces of grief weigh heavy on the heart. Silence serves to lift up the mourner's heart and create much-needed space to give attention to the grief. Being in silence helps restore energy and inspires courage to explore the many facets of transformational grief.

## What Silence Can Teach

In choosing to companion instead of treating people in grief, you choose a way of being that values and gives honor to silence. You bring a sensitivity to the importance of listening first. You give attention to the mourner's deepest needs. You acknowledge her uniqueness. You embrace her life force and marry hope to your quiet soul. You silence any instinct to make judgments in your head and you stay connected to your heart. You feel your own emotions as you sit in the stillness and stay in search of a desire to be taught by the mourner. When you do respond, you do it in a considerate and compassionate way that recognizes the vulnerable soul that you are ministering to.

As someone who sits with people in silence, you recognize that so much about grief is a mystery that doesn't lend itself to words. You stand at the graveside with parents who have just experienced the death of their precious child and words are inadequate. You bend down to touch the child whose mother has just died in a tragic auto accident and words are inadequate. The sadness of loss hangs in a wistful silence. Once again you are humbled by an awareness that deep understanding of the ways of life and death cannot be expressed in words.

# Tenet Eight

Companioning is about being still; it is not about frantic movement forward.

*"Things come suitable to their time."* —Enid Bagnold

Many of the messages that people in grief are given are in opposition to stillness… "carry on;" "keep your chin up;" "keep busy;" "I have someone for you to meet." Yet, the paradox for many grievers is that as they try to frantically move forward, they often lose their way.

*"There is more to life than merely increasing its speed."* —Gandhi

As a companion, your capacity to be still with the mourner will help her honor the deeper voices of quiet wisdom. As Rainer Maria Rilke observed, "Everything is gestation and then bringing forth." In honoring stillness, you help the mourner rest for the journey.

Times of stillness are not anchored in a psychological need but in a spiritual necessity. A lack of stillness hastens confusion and disorientation and results in a waning of the spirit. If the mourner does not rest in stillness, she cannot and will not find her way out of the wilderness of grief. Stillness allows for movement from soul work to spirit work; it restores the life force.

Within the sanctuary of stillness, discernment that is bathed in grace and wisdom is born. Thus, one of my mantras as a caregiver is, "Go slow; there are no rewards for speed." Grief is only transformed when we honor the quiet forces of stillness.

## Without Stillness

Without stillness the mourner cannot create the energy needed to embrace the work of mourning. In sitting with suffering in stillness, you make yourself available for those you companion to give voice to their grief. You become present to the insight and wisdom that come forth only out of stillness. It's as if the stillness invites the head to settle gently in the heart.

Without stillness, the mourner lacks a foundation from which to, eventually, transform grief into renewed meaning and purpose. The mourner needs stillness to encounter the full force of the powerful nature of grief. Out of the stillness often comes the inspiration to be respectful of grief, to seek the wisdom of those who have gone before.

Observation has taught me that the integration of grief is borne out of stillness, not frantic movement forward. By saying no to the use of techniques to try to "make something happen," sacred space arises for things to happen; Divine

Momentum is set in motion. When we stop managing grief, other things such as grace, wisdom, love, and truth come forth.

In honoring stillness as a companion to someone in grief, you discover that spiritual forces evolve that discourage striving and encourage rest and eventual renewal. Attempting to consciously move forward, or worse yet, making any attempt to get him to "let go," becomes counterproductive. Frantic movement forward depletes an already naturally malnourished soul. It is through stillness that one's soul is ever so slowly restored.

> *"The rhythm of stillness is the teacher of contentment and peace."*
> —Gabriella Roth

> *"The wounds of the past must be tended by more than the frantic activity of 'getting on with it.'"*
> —Oriah Mountain Dreamer

## Stillness and Pain

As a companion, you will be well served to focus your heart's attention on the importance of stillness in relation to pain and suffering. If you do not perceive value in the role of pain in healing, it will be all but impossible to be still with people in grief.

If you in any way perceive the pain of grief as unnecessary or inappropriate, you will be reluctant to be in the stillness. In stillness, you come face to face with the essence of grief and raw feelings of loss and profound sadness. At times, you will confront the dark night of the soul—a profound sense of spiritual deprivation wherein the person you are companioning may well question the very desire to go on living.

If you do not see that it is in hurting that we ultimately heal, you will greet stillness with anxiety and fear. Fearful of what you might find in the stillness, you will instinctually push stillness away, keeping yourself and the mourner busy with techniques intended to avoid the depth of a multitude of feelings. In stillness,

*"I learned the interior life was as rewarding as the exterior life and that my richest moments occurred when I was absolutely still."*
—Richard Bode

*"I never found a companion that was as companionable as solitude."*
—Henry David Thoreau

as you stop and listen, you will hear and feel the emptiness that accompanies grief.

By contrast, if you surrender to the reality that pain and suffering are part of the healing journey, you can sit with the stillness. You can step back from any urge to fix the pain. You can appreciate and trust that out of the darkness will eventually come the light. You will see the underlying strength and wisdom that are borne out of respect for the stillness. You will come to see that it is out of the stillness that the person discovers that authentic mourning invites the blessings of living fully each and every day.

# Tenet Nine

## Companioning is about respecting disorder and confusion; it is not about imposing order and logic.

*"Instead of struggling against the force of confusion, we could meet it and relax."* —Pema Chodron

The death of someone loved brings about significant change in the life of the mourner. Change of any kind starts with disorder and confusion. Companioning is not about

understanding the disorder and confusion, figuring it out, or trying to make it better.

*"A deep distress has humanized my soul."*
—William Wordsworth

The challenge for the companion is to stay present to the disorientation, and trust that the natural unfolding process will eventually result in re-orientation. When it comes to matters of the soul, the last thing the mourner needs is to be joined at the head level. When disoriented and confused, he needs companions at the heart level. If you can give up the hope that disorder and confusion can be quickly and efficiently moved away from, then you can help the mourner be more self-compassionate and not feel such urging to be rid of these normal symptoms of the journey.

## The Disorder of Grief

Disorder and confusion is a time of waiting, a time of paralysis, a time when the world doesn't make sense in the way it did before the death. The mourner may experience a sense of restlessness, agitation, impatience, and ongoing confusion.

There is often an inability to complete tasks. The mourner is often forgetful and everyday pleasures may not seem to matter right now.

The mourner may experience a restless searching for the person who died. This searching and yearning can leave her feeling drained and can be accompanied by the "lethargy of grief." These are only a few of many care-eliciting symptoms the mourner may have when experiencing disorder and confusion.

The unfortunate reality is that many grievers do not give themselves permission to surrender to or relax into their disorder and confusion. We live in a society that often encourages the repression or denial of any kind of disorder and confusion, and in its place we impose order and logic: "You just need to get a hold of yourself and get on with life. Being upset isn't going to change anything." The result of this is

*"I wanted a perfect ending. Now I've learned, the hard way, that some poems don't rhyme, and some stories don't have a clear beginning, middle, and end. Life is about not knowing, having to change, taking the moment and making the best of it, without knowing what's going to happen next. Delicious Ambiguity."* —Gilda Radner

that many people either grieve in isolation or attempt to run away from their grief through various means, including order and logic.

## Using Logic to Order Grief

While there are a number of unique ways by which people repress, deny, or move away from the disorienting symptoms of grief, I will limit my discussion here to the minimizer/ intellectualizer who tries to use order and logic to overcome grief. This person is usually very sensitive to feelings of disorder and confusion, but when he feels them, he works to minimize them by diluting them through a variety of rationalizations.

This person often attempts to prove to himself that he is not really impacted by the loss. Observers of the minimizer/ intellectualizer may hear him talk about how well he is doing and how he is back to his normal routine. On a conscious level his logic may seem to be working and certainly conforms to society's message to quickly "get over" one's grief. However, internally the repressed feelings of grief build and emotional and spiritual strain—soul symptoms—result.

This person often believes (often because of unconscious contamination by a mourning-avoidant culture) that grief is something to be thought through but not felt through. This is typically an intellectual process in which words become a substitute for the expression of authentic feelings. Any disorder and confusion is threatening to the minimizer/intellectualizer, who seeks to avoid feeling a loss of control. Worse yet, she might find an "expert" counselor who shares these beliefs and tries to use techniques to overcome the disorder and confusion.

*"The truth is that our finest moments are most likely to occur when we are feeling deeply uncomfortable, unhappy, or unfulfilled. For it is only in such moments, propelled by our discomfort, that we are likely to step out of our ruts and start searching for different ways or truer answers."* —M. Scott Peck

Unfortunately, the more this person works to convince herself that the feelings of grief have been overcome, the more crippled she becomes in allowing for emotional and spiritual expression. The result is often a destructive, vicious cycle.

In my experience, the need for the mourner to stay logical and orderly is usually a problem in allowing oneself to feel and express deep feelings. Some people struggle with a high need for self-control, others may have an intolerance for experiences of disorder and confusion accompanied by pain and helplessness, while still others may lack a support system that encourages the expression of their feelings.

Yes, the disorder and confusion that accompany grief can be overwhelming to the mourner. When she is encountering this disorientation, everything in her may want to shut down. Yet, in the process she may be tempted to shut out precisely what she needs. She may see the disorder and confusion as the enemy.

As a companion, you, on the other hand, realize that there is no enemy and that these symptoms are the result of being torn apart by grief. The disorder is a biofeedback mechanism

*"Have patience with everything that remains unsolved in your heart. Try to love the questions themselves, like locked rooms and like books written in a foreign language. Do not now look for the answers. They cannot now be given to you because you could not live them. It is a question of experiencing everything. At present you need to live the question. Perhaps you will gradually, without even noticing it, find yourself experiencing the answer, some distant day."* —Rainer Maria Rilke

reminding the mourner to stay open to the loss. Now the question becomes: how will she host the disorder and confusion? Will she try to will it away through order and logic, or will she be patient and self-nurturing and seek the support of compassionate companions?

Without doubt, one of the reasons many people are preoccupied with the question, "How long does grief last?" has to do with society's impatience with grief. Persons who continue to express grief are often viewed as "weak," "crazy," or "self-pitying." Grief is something to be overcome instead of experienced.

The result of these kinds of messages is the adoption of rational, mechanistic principles of order and logic to defend against disorder and confusion. Refusal to allow tears, suffering in silence, and "being strong" are thought to be admirable behaviors. Yet, the most helpful approach to grief is to approach it head-on and honor the value of symptoms that reflect special needs.

## The Silent Mourner

The lack of expression of outward mourning has brought about the evolution of the "silent mourner." Even those who want to be supportive cannot identify this mourner. The relegating of grief to behind closed doors reinforces the importance of being outreach-oriented in your companioning efforts.

All too often, our society fails to support mourners who suffer from soul-based symptoms of disorder and confusion. An emphasis on being rational and under control influences mourners to reintegrate into the social network and keep their tears, fears, and pains to themselves. As a responsible rebel, I invite you to join me in an effort to reverse this trend that fails to acknowledge the need for compassion and support to people who experience normal symptoms of disorder and confusion of grief. Supporting people in grief is about love; it is not about logic!

# Tenet Ten

## Companioning is about learning from others; it is not about teaching them.

*"Allow stories to be told without slipping into interpretations, analysis, and conclusions."* —Thomas Moore

When I attended graduate school in traditional psychology, I learned semantics such as *assess*, *diagnose*, and *treat*. In large part, I was taught to study a body of knowledge surrounding mental health, assume expert status as a professional, and treat people as patients. Yes, I was taught a catalog of disorders and standard interventions based on the assumption that I had made an accurate diagnosis. What I later came to call my "unconscious contamination" had me believing I was responsible for the cure. It was only through time, maturation, and experience that I came to reject this model of caregiving.

Walking with thousands of people in grief has resulted in an "educated heart" that has led me to accept my role as a responsible rebel. I learned the medical model of mental health care, but my real life experiences caused me to reject it in favor of a companioning model of caregiving. As I noted in the Introduction, I believe that our modern understanding of grief lacks an appreciation for and attention to the spiritual, soulful nature of the grief journey.

*"Healers are hosts who patiently and carefully listen to the story of the suffering strangers."*
—Henri Nouwen

I have left my clinical doctoring behind to become the companion I am today. As a companion, I believe that grief is organic. Grief is as natural as the setting of the sun and as elemental as gravity. Grief is a complex but perfectly natural—and necessary—mixture of human emotions. Companions do not cure mourners; instead, we create conditions that allow them to teach us. Our ministry is more art than science, more heart than head. The bereaved person is not our patient but instead our companion.

## Support Groups and Stories

In North America today, thousands of people find this kind of companionship in grief support groups. The worth of these programs certainly does not emanate from empirically supported treatments, but from something much more simple (yet powerful): the telling of stories. The meetings are anchored in honoring each member's stories of grief and supporting each other's need to authentically mourn. No effort is made to interpret or analyze. The group affirms the storyteller for the courage to express the raw wounds that often accompany loss.

*"Stories, carefully chosen and shaped by both the teller and the listener, can open gateways into our interior landscape, can reveal the meaning in our lives enfolded in the details and unfolded in their telling and conscious contemplation."*
—Oriah Mountain Dreamer

The stories speak the truth. The stories create hope. The stories create healing.

Effective leaders of such groups come to recognize that their role is not so much about group counseling techniques as it is about creating "sacred space" in the group so that each person's story can be nonjudgmentally received. Effective grief group leadership is a humble yet demanding role of creating this space in ways that members can express their wounds in the body of community. The very experience of telling one's story in the common bond of the group contradicts the isolation and shame that characterizes so many people's lives in a mourning-avoidant culture. And, because stories of love and loss take time, patience, and unconditional love, they serve as powerful antidotes to a modern society that is all too often preoccupied with getting people to "let go" and "move on."

The creation of new meaning and purpose in life requires that mourners "re-story" their lives. Obviously, this calls out for the need for empathetic companions, not treaters. Indigenous cultures acknowledge that honoring stories helps reshape a person's experience. The stories are reshaped not in the telling of the story once or twice or even three times, but over and over again. Mourners need compassionate listeners to hear and affirm their truths. So, as a companion, your upholding of people's stories allows you the privilege of being a "shapeshifter"!

The many benefits of honoring the stories of our fellow human beings include:

- We can search for wholeness among our fractured parts.
- We can come to know who we are in new and unexpected ways.
- We can explore our past and come to a more profound understanding of our origins and our future directions.
- We can tentatively explain our view of the world and come to understand who we are.
- We can explore how love experienced and love lost have influenced our time on earth.
- We can discover that a life without story is like a book without pages—nice to see but lacking in substance.
- We can seek forgiveness and be humbled by our mortality.
- We can determine how adversity has enriched our meaning and purpose in life.
- We can journey inward and discover connections previously not understood or acknowledged.

- We can create an awareness of how the past interfaces with the present, and how the present ebbs back into the past.

- We can discover that the route to healing lies not only in the physical realm, but also in the emotional and spiritual realms.

- We can find that the fulfillment of a life well lived is bestowed through the translation of our past into experiences that are expressed through the oral or written word.

- We can realize that the true significance of each unique story is that you can capture the spirit, the soul, and the genuine worth of the person who has died.

- We can come to understand that in our pain and suffering lies the awareness of the preciousness of each day on the earth.

- We can discover our truth in this present moment of time and space.

## Honoring Our Own Stories

I believe that mourners can instinctively sense who can listen to their stories and who cannot. They often look for signs of open-heartedness and will gladly tell their stories to those they sense have a receptive spirit. The capacity to attend to your own stories of loss allows you to open your heart and connect to other people's stories.

Honoring stories, both our own and others', requires that we slow down, turn inward, and create the sacred space to do so. Yes, this can be

*"Telling a story, especially about ourselves, can be one of the most personal and intimate things we can do."* —Richard Stone

challenging in a fast-paced, efficiency-based culture in which many people lack an understanding of the value of telling the story.

Yet, companions realize that it is in having places to re-story their lives that they can embrace what needs to be embraced and come to understand that the human spirit prevails. We heal ourselves as we tell the tale. This is the awesome power of story.

# Tenet Eleven

## Companioning is about compassionate curiosity; it is not about expertise.

*"Real understanding is a creative mixture of certainty and unknowing. The trick is to know when you don't understand."* —Thomas Moore

Curiosity for the companion is about being willing to enter into and learn about the mystery of grief while recognizing you do not and cannot fully understand someone else's experience. Curiosity is bathed in an attitude that Zen calls the "beginner's mind" or "know-nothing mind."

This attitude is not ignorance but the capacity to see without assumptions, to take a fresh look each and every time you are privileged to walk with and learn from a mourner. It involves a clearing away of thoughts, beliefs, and ideas that might cloud your ability to see things as they are in pristine form.

As we all realize, children are naturally curious. As we grow up we are at risk for losing this state of heightened awareness and natural desire to learn from those around us. We may falsely assume we already know. In other words, our intellect takes over. Yet, being a companion to people in grief can reactivate

*"Listening for and being curious about client competencies, resources, and resiliencies does not mean that the therapist ignores the client's pain or assumes a cheerleading attitude. Rather, it requires that the therapist listen to the whole story; the confusion and the clarity, the suffering and the endurance, the pain and the coping, the desperation and the desire."*
—From *The Heroic Client*, by Barry Duncan and Scott Miller

our sense of miracle to bring a fresh, simple, unsophisticated view of things.

## You Don't Know

Paradoxically, you can only learn from the mourner by acknowledging you don't know. It is out of your helplessness that you ultimately become helpful. You have to be willing to disconnect from believing you have superior expertise of another human being's emotional-spiritual journey of grief.

Through no fault of your own, your training as a caregiver may make it difficult to admit you don't know and don't have answers. You may instinctively be frightened to be present to people who are in liminal space—betwixt and between!

Actually, you may have been taught that part of being a professional is to project confidence and to state opinions as if they were gospel. You don't get respected in this culture by admitting you are confused or by asking

*"Communities of like-minded people develop beliefs and practices, teach them to each other, reinforce them as the standard beliefs of the community, and lose sight of the fact that those beliefs and practices are their own make-do creations."*
—Robert T. Fancher

tentative questions in search of enhancing your empathy versus providing techniques for brief therapy that collaborate with managed care. The unconscious contamination of your training is more likely to encourage you to assess, diagnose, and treat than it is to observe, witness, listen, learn, and watch out for the mourner.

For some caregivers it is difficult, if not impossible, to relinquish their "diagnostic categories," "interventions," and "treatments." These terms often lie at the heart of the professional identity of the caregiver and the attempt to be part of the medical model of expertise. Yet, the companion humbly acknowledges that "compassionate curiosity" is what you really need to care for the mourner.

You have the honor as a companion to listen and to learn, to be curious rather than to be certain. The greatest privilege of the companioning model, in fact, is that it moves you closer to the very people you wish to support. When you listen without a need to judge or interpret, you create a safe place and become a safe person for the mourner.

**Compassionate curiosity**
Actively encouraging the mourner to teach you about her grief while you remain patient, humble, and caring.

At bottom, it is not our differences that divide us. Instead, it is our judgments about each other that do. Curiosity and use of the "teach me" model bring us back together. To use this model invites us to rest in the sometimes uncomfortable place of uncertainty of not knowing, having the answer, or being the expert. Companioning invites you to pay attention to the soul work and spirit work and to be led rather than to lead.

## The Myth of the Expert

Today, more and more caregivers are seeking certification as grief educators, counselors, and therapists. My own Center for Loss and Life Transition offers a certificate in Death and Grief Studies. Yet I want to be clear that the receiving of this certificate following 150 hours of reflection on the mystery of death and grief doesn't make the recipient an expert. Actually, it means the person has been willing to ponder the mysteries and learn to be curious when learning from the true expert—the mourner! To be perceived, or worse yet, to perceive oneself, as an expert grief counselor may be the first step toward unbecoming a creative companion.

A Buddhist teaching notes, "In the beginner's mind there are many possibilities; in the expert's mind there are few." One astute observer of this reality was Bradford Keeney, who wrote the following about the hazards of being an expert or master counselor: "You will find that it no longer matters what you say. Everything uttered will be contextualized as the voice of a master... Avoid the political posturings of 'mastery' and return to embracing and cultivating a beginner's mind. Maintain and respect ignorance. Speak to hear the surprise from your own voice."

As you contemplate the value of curiosity versus expertise, listen to your own inner voice. What has your own personal grief taught you about what helps people heal? Have you witnessed change as the journey unfolds, but not according to plan or as a consequence of intentional intervention? Do you appreciate the mystery of grief and challenge the wish to have it resolved (which it can never be)? Do you believe that caring for the mourner requires a different language than that of modern academic psychology? Depending on your answers, you may have to admit you are a responsible rebel who believes in compassionate curiosity and challenges ego-based expertise.

I believe that every counselor must work to develop his or her own theory or point of view about what helps bereaved people heal. Challenging yourself to explain what happens in your counseling relationships with bereaved people and families will, in my experience, assist you in understanding and improving the work you do to assist those you desire to companion.

Developing your own tenets encourages a coherence of ideas about the helping process and generates new ideas about how to be helpful. Now that you've read about my tenets of companioning the bereaved, I hope you will give thought to yours.

*"The great danger of the increasing professionalization of the different forms of healing is that they become ways of exercising power instead of offering service."* —Henri Nouwen

# A Final Word

*"We use the expression 'creating a space for others'
to mean that the counselor is ready to be hospitable to
the person he or she hopes to help."* —Janet Kornfeld

## Companioning as a Reflection of Love

At the very heart of companioning is the need to
acknowledge each other as equals, not as "therapist"
and "patient." What makes us all equals is that we are
all human beings who will come to know the pain and
suffering that emanate from the loss of those we have
loved. We also need each other.

Companioning can only take place among equals. If
anyone believes she has superior knowledge of another's
journey into grief, this belief destroys the foundation
of a relationship anchored in unconditional love. Those
who project what I call "superior expertise" can't help
but "treat" the mourner, and usually—consciously
or unconsciously—try to achieve some variation of
"closure." When we see each other as equals, we do not

misuse each other. Acknowledging each other as equals is a reflection of love.

Companioning is also about compassionate curiosity. When we support each other with this humility, we open our hearts to another human being. Curiosity encourages us to take off our professional masks and create sacred, hospitable free space for the mourner. It takes time and conscious effort to create this space in a mourning-avoidant culture. Compassionate curiosity encourages us to extend ourselves rather than withdraw into our own worlds. Yes, companioning invites us to extend ourselves, open our hearts wide, be still and really listen.

Companioning also depends on our willingness to reject grief as a pathology and not think of our role as eradicating emotional and spiritual suffering. We must surrender to the wilderness to be willing to wander into the mystery. We have to expect chaos, confusion, disorder, and even despair. So-called "negative" emotions and experiences are not dangerous. Messiness has its place. Grief loss and change always start with confusion. We can't be companions if we refuse to be confused.

Integration of loss often occurs in the space of not knowing. We don't need to be joined at the head with a mourner; we need to be joined at the heart.

In recent years, in attempting to explain the complexities of grief, we have seen the evolution of the field of thanatology, which is the study of death and dying. I myself am a "certified thanatologist." But it seems that in the effort to create another field of expertise, we have witnessed a dramatic movement away from our philosophical roots as caregivers. The ancient philosophers were always conscious of the need to explore the whole of the human body, mind, spirit, and soul. They stayed open to the mystery and did not research representative control groups.

In the 1900s, psychology created an alliance with the Newtonian model of science and broke away from philosophy and the arts. Yet, the human spirit impacted by loss is intertwined with the voices of the soul, the avenue through which inner turmoil and grief are experienced and brought from dark into light.

We might be well served to ask some of the following questions:

- Where do grief and sadness go when we as a society no longer honor the depth of feelings of loss and relegate the care of the mourner to the "specialist" who is at risk for "treating" what are actually normal and necessary soul-based symptoms of mourning?

- What happens when we live in a society where feelings of grief are seen as signs of weakness instead of signs of strength? What happens to people in need of unconditional support when they are perceived as "immature" or "overly emotional"?

- Have many people in our society come to believe that feelings of grief are unnecessary and inappropriate? How does this influence their ability to seek and accept support in the face of loss?

- What happens to mourners when many people around them are projecting a desire for "resolution" or "closure"?

- What happens when a society forgets that saying hello to our dead is the pathway to goodbye?

- What happens when "solution-oriented" and "brief, cognitive" therapies and "managed care" become popular and confuse efficiency with effectiveness?

- What happens in society when it seems more important to get people back to work just three days after the death of someone loved than it is to restore their souls?

- What happens when a society cannot slow down and be still in ways that allow the understanding of the head to settle gently in the heart?

- What happens when a society loses an understanding that the symptoms that come with being "torn apart" by grief are biofeedback mechanisms reminding the mourner to stay open to the loss?

- What happens when a society moves from the front porch to the back porch and loses an understanding of the need to "re-story" the life of the mourner?

- Would a society less inhibited in personal expressions of loss and suffering have less need for acting-out in violence against those who act out against us? In other words, does our inability to mourn openly and authentically impact our tendency to want to strike out at others in the face of loss?

- Do we as caregivers realize that to stand in the midst of another human being's pain and suffering requires that we befriend our own pain and suffering? In other words, do we understand that we cannot companion people into the wilderness unless we are willing to go there ourselves?

Every day we each have the opportunity to be companions, to listen with our hearts, and to be curious rather than certain. Thank you so much for taking time to read this book. I hope you choose to see your heart opening to people experiencing grief. When your heart is open, you are receptive to what life brings you, both happy and sad. By "staying open," you create a pathway to living life fully until you die.

Thank you, too, for sharing the companioning care model with others. Just imagine how profoundly the world would change if all those who mourn life's losses—everyone!—were compassionately companioned through their grief journeys. By discussing the companioning philosophy, sharing this book, and even taking classes at my Center for Loss so that you can return home to train others in your community, you will be joining me in my mission to help people mourn well, so they can go on to live well and love well.

Bless you and Godspeed.

---

**Bring Dr. Wolfelt to your community!**

One of today's most respected and popular educators, Dr. Wolfelt presents workshops on grief-related topics— including the art of companioning—to both laypeople and professional caregivers throughout North America. If you are interested in sponsoring a workshop in your area, please call the Center for Loss at (970) 226-6050 or e-mail Dr. Wolfelt at DrWolfelt@centerforloss.com.

**Attend one of Dr. Wolfelt's retreat-oriented learning experiences at the Center for Loss!**

In Fort Collins, Colorado, near the beautiful Rocky Mountain foothills, Dr. Wolfelt teaches four-day, small group learning retreats for grief caregivers. Visit www.centerforloss.com for the upcoming schedule.

---

# ALSO BY ALAN WOLFELT

## Companioning the Bereaved
### A Soulful Guide for Caregivers

This book by one of North America's most respected grief educators presents a model for grief counseling based on his "companioning" principles.

For many mental healthcare providers, grief in contemporary society has been medicalized—perceived as if it were an illness that with proper assessment, diagnosis, and treatment could be cured.

Dr. Wolfelt explains that our modern understanding of grief all too often conveys that at bereavement's "end" the mourner has completed a series of tasks, extinguished pain, and established new relationships. Our psychological models emphasize "recovery" or "resolution" in grief, suggesting a return to "normalcy."

Beyond a discussion of the companioning philosophy of grief care, this book contains 100 additional pages that explore Dr. Wolfelt's "wisdom teachings"—including the influences on each mourner's unique journey and the six central needs of mourning.

ISBN 978-1-879651-41-8 • hardcover • 176 pages • $29.95

## Companioning the Dying
### A Soulful Guide for Caregivers

#### by Greg Yoder
#### Foreword by Alan D. Wolfelt, Ph.D.

Based on the assumption that all dying experiences belong not to the caregivers but to those who are dying—and that there is no such thing as a "good death" or a "bad death," *Companioning the Dying* helps readers bring a respectful, nonjudgmental presence to the dying while liberating them from self-imposed or popular expectations to say or do the right thing.

Written with candor and wit by hospice counselor Greg Yoder (who has companioned several hundred dying people and their families), *Companioning the Dying* exudes a compassion and a clarity that can only come from intimate work with the dying. The book teaches through real-life stories that will resonate with both experienced clinical professionals as well as laypeople in the throes of caring for a dying loved one.

ISBN 978-1-879651-42-5 • hardcover • 176 pages • $29.95

# ALSO BY ALAN WOLFELT

## The Wilderness of Grief
### Finding Your Way

A beautiful, hardcover gift book version of
*Understanding Your Grief*

*Understanding Your Grief* provides a comprehensive exploration of grief and the ten essential touchstones for finding hope and healing your heart. *The Wilderness of Grief* is an excerpted version of *Understanding Your Grief*, making it approachable and appropriate for all mourners.

This concise book makes an excellent gift for anyone in mourning. On the book's inside front cover is room for writing an inscription to your grieving friend.

*The Wilderness of Grief* is an ideal book for the bedside or coffee table. Pick it up before bed and read just a few pages. You'll be carried off to sleep by its gentle, affirming messages of hope and healing.

ISBN 978-1-879651-52-4 • 128 pages • hardcover • $15.95

## The Journey Through Grief
### Reflections On Healing
### Second Edition

This popular hardcover book makes a wonderful gift for those who grieve, helping them gently engage in the work of mourning. Comforting and nurturing, *The Journey Through Grief* doses mourners with the six needs of mourning, helping them soothe themselves at the same time it helps them heal.

This revised, second edition of *The Journey Through Grief* takes Dr. Wolfelt's popular book of reflections and adds space for guided journaling, asking readers thoughtful questions about their unique mourning needs and providing room to write responses.

*The Journey Through Grief* is organized around the six needs that all mourners must yield to—indeed embrace—if they are to go on to find continued meaning in life and living. Following a short explanation of each mourning need is a series of brief, spiritual passages that, when read slowly and reflectively, help mourners work through their unique thoughts and feelings. *The Journey Through Grief* is being used by many faith communities as part of their grief support programs.

ISBN 978-1-879651-11-1 • hardcover • 176 pages • $21.95